THIS PASSWORD BOOK BELONGS TO:

_____

WEBSITE:

E-MAIL:

USERNAME:

PASSWORD:

NOTES:

WEBSITE:

E-MAIL:

USERNAME:

PASSWORD:

NOTES:

WEBSITE:

E-MAIL:

USERNAME:

PASSWORD:

NOTES:

WEBSITE:

E-MAIL:

USERNAME:

PASSWORD:

NOTES:

WEBSITE:

E-MAIL:

USERNAME:

PASSWORD:

NOTES:

WEBSITE:

E-MAIL:

USERNAME:

PASSWORD:

NOTES:

WEBSITE:

E-MAIL:

USERNAME:

PASSWORD:

NOTES:

WEBSITE:

E-MAIL:

USERNAME:

PASSWORD:

NOTES:

WEBSITE:

E-MAIL:

USERNAME:

PASSWORD:

NOTES:

WEBSITE:

E-MAIL:

USERNAME:

PASSWORD:

NOTES:

WEBSITE:

E-MAIL:

USERNAME:

PASSWORD:

NOTES:

WEBSITE:

E-MAIL:

USERNAME:

PASSWORD:

NOTES:

WEBSITE:

E-MAIL:

USERNAME:

PASSWORD:

NOTES:

WEBSITE:

E-MAIL:

USERNAME:

PASSWORD:

NOTES:

WEBSITE:

E-MAIL:

USERNAME:

PASSWORD:

NOTES:

WEBSITE:

E-MAIL:

USERNAME:

PASSWORD:

NOTES:

WEBSITE:

E-MAIL:

USERNAME:

PASSWORD:

NOTES:

WEBSITE:

E-MAIL:

USERNAME:

PASSWORD:

NOTES:

WEBSITE:

E-MAIL:

USERNAME:

PASSWORD:

NOTES:

WEBSITE:

E-MAIL:

USERNAME:

PASSWORD:

NOTES:

WEBSITE:

E-MAIL:

USERNAME:

PASSWORD:

NOTES:

WEBSITE:

E-MAIL:

USERNAME:

PASSWORD:

NOTES:

WEBSITE:

E-MAIL:

USERNAME:

PASSWORD:

NOTES:

WEBSITE:

E-MAIL:

USERNAME:

PASSWORD:

NOTES:

WEBSITE:

E-MAIL:

USERNAME:

PASSWORD:

NOTES:

WEBSITE:

E-MAIL:

USERNAME:

PASSWORD:

NOTES:

WEBSITE:

E-MAIL:

USERNAME:

PASSWORD:

NOTES:

WEBSITE:

E-MAIL:

USERNAME:

PASSWORD:

NOTES:

WEBSITE:

E-MAIL:

USERNAME:

PASSWORD:

NOTES:

WEBSITE:

E-MAIL:

USERNAME:

PASSWORD:

NOTES:

WEBSITE:

E-MAIL:

USERNAME:

PASSWORD:

NOTES:

WEBSITE:

E-MAIL:

USERNAME:

PASSWORD:

NOTES:

WEBSITE:

E-MAIL:

USERNAME:

PASSWORD:

NOTES:

WEBSITE:

E-MAIL:

USERNAME:

PASSWORD:

NOTES:

WEBSITE:

E-MAIL:

USERNAME:

PASSWORD:

NOTES:

WEBSITE:

E-MAIL:

USERNAME:

PASSWORD:

NOTES:

WEBSITE:

E-MAIL:

USERNAME:

PASSWORD:

NOTES:

WEBSITE:

E-MAIL:

USERNAME:

PASSWORD:

NOTES:

WEBSITE:

E-MAIL:

USERNAME:

PASSWORD:

NOTES:

WEBSITE:

E-MAIL:

USERNAME:

PASSWORD:

NOTES:

WEBSITE:

E-MAIL:

USERNAME:

PASSWORD:

NOTES:

WEBSITE:

E-MAIL:

USERNAME:

PASSWORD:

NOTES:

WEBSITE:

E-MAIL:

USERNAME:

PASSWORD:

NOTES:

WEBSITE:

E-MAIL:

USERNAME:

PASSWORD:

NOTES:

WEBSITE:

E-MAIL:

USERNAME:

PASSWORD:

NOTES:

WEBSITE:

E-MAIL:

USERNAME:

PASSWORD:

NOTES:

WEBSITE:

E-MAIL:

USERNAME:

PASSWORD:

NOTES:

WEBSITE:

E-MAIL:

USERNAME:

PASSWORD:

NOTES:

WEBSITE:

E-MAIL:

USERNAME:

PASSWORD:

NOTES:

WEBSITE:

E-MAIL:

USERNAME:

PASSWORD:

NOTES:

WEBSITE:

E-MAIL:

USERNAME:

PASSWORD:

NOTES:

WEBSITE:

E-MAIL:

USERNAME:

PASSWORD:

NOTES:

WEBSITE:

E-MAIL:

USERNAME:

PASSWORD:

NOTES:

WEBSITE:

E-MAIL:

USERNAME:

PASSWORD:

NOTES:

WEBSITE:

E-MAIL:

USERNAME:

PASSWORD:

NOTES:

WEBSITE:

E-MAIL:

USERNAME:

PASSWORD:

NOTES:

WEBSITE:

E-MAIL:

USERNAME:

PASSWORD:

NOTES:

WEBSITE:

E-MAIL:

USERNAME:

PASSWORD:

NOTES:

WEBSITE:

E-MAIL:

USERNAME:

PASSWORD:

NOTES:

WEBSITE:

E-MAIL:

USERNAME:

PASSWORD:

NOTES:

WEBSITE:

E-MAIL:

USERNAME:

PASSWORD:

NOTES:

WEBSITE:

E-MAIL:

USERNAME:

PASSWORD:

NOTES:

WEBSITE:

E-MAIL:

USERNAME:

PASSWORD:

NOTES:

WEBSITE:

E-MAIL:

USERNAME:

PASSWORD:

NOTES:

WEBSITE:

E-MAIL:

USERNAME:

PASSWORD:

NOTES:

WEBSITE:

E-MAIL:

USERNAME:

PASSWORD:

NOTES:

WEBSITE:

E-MAIL:

USERNAME:

PASSWORD:

NOTES:

WEBSITE:

E-MAIL:

USERNAME:

PASSWORD:

NOTES:

WEBSITE:

E-MAIL:

USERNAME:

PASSWORD:

NOTES:

WEBSITE:

E-MAIL:

USERNAME:

PASSWORD:

NOTES:

WEBSITE:

E-MAIL:

USERNAME:

PASSWORD:

NOTES:

WEBSITE:

E-MAIL:

USERNAME:

PASSWORD:

NOTES:

WEBSITE:

E-MAIL:

USERNAME:

PASSWORD:

NOTES:

WEBSITE:

E-MAIL:

USERNAME:

PASSWORD:

NOTES:

WEBSITE:

E-MAIL:

USERNAME:

PASSWORD:

NOTES:

WEBSITE:

E-MAIL:

USERNAME:

PASSWORD:

NOTES:

WEBSITE:

E-MAIL:

USERNAME:

PASSWORD:

NOTES:

WEBSITE:

E-MAIL:

USERNAME:

PASSWORD:

NOTES:

WEBSITE:

E-MAIL:

USERNAME:

PASSWORD:

NOTES:

WEBSITE:

E-MAIL:

USERNAME:

PASSWORD:

NOTES:

WEBSITE:

E-MAIL:

USERNAME:

PASSWORD:

NOTES:

WEBSITE:

E-MAIL:

USERNAME:

PASSWORD:

NOTES:

WEBSITE:

E-MAIL:

USERNAME:

PASSWORD:

NOTES:

WEBSITE:

E-MAIL:

USERNAME:

PASSWORD:

NOTES:

WEBSITE:

E-MAIL:

USERNAME:

PASSWORD:

NOTES:

WEBSITE:

E-MAIL:

USERNAME:

PASSWORD:

NOTES:

WEBSITE:

E-MAIL:

USERNAME:

PASSWORD:

NOTES:

WEBSITE:

E-MAIL:

USERNAME:

PASSWORD:

NOTES:

WEBSITE:

E-MAIL:

USERNAME:

PASSWORD:

NOTES:

WEBSITE:

E-MAIL:

USERNAME:

PASSWORD:

NOTES:

WEBSITE:

E-MAIL:

USERNAME:

PASSWORD:

NOTES:

WEBSITE:

E-MAIL:

USERNAME:

PASSWORD:

NOTES:

WEBSITE:

E-MAIL:

USERNAME:

PASSWORD:

NOTES:

WEBSITE:

E-MAIL:

USERNAME:

PASSWORD:

NOTES:

WEBSITE:

E-MAIL:

USERNAME:

PASSWORD:

NOTES:

WEBSITE:

E-MAIL:

USERNAME:

PASSWORD:

NOTES:

WEBSITE:

E-MAIL:

USERNAME:

PASSWORD:

NOTES:

WEBSITE:

E-MAIL:

USERNAME:

PASSWORD:

NOTES:

WEBSITE:

E-MAIL:

USERNAME:

PASSWORD:

NOTES:

WEBSITE:

E-MAIL:

USERNAME:

PASSWORD:

NOTES:

WEBSITE:

E-MAIL:

USERNAME:

PASSWORD:

NOTES:

WEBSITE:

E-MAIL:

USERNAME:

PASSWORD:

NOTES:

WEBSITE:

E-MAIL:

USERNAME:

PASSWORD:

NOTES:

WEBSITE:

E-MAIL:

USERNAME:

PASSWORD:

NOTES:

WEBSITE:

E-MAIL:

USERNAME:

PASSWORD:

NOTES:

WEBSITE:

E-MAIL:

USERNAME:

PASSWORD:

NOTES:

WEBSITE:

E-MAIL:

USERNAME:

PASSWORD:

NOTES:

WEBSITE:

E-MAIL:

USERNAME:

PASSWORD:

NOTES:

WEBSITE:

E-MAIL:

USERNAME:

PASSWORD:

NOTES:

WEBSITE:

E-MAIL:

USERNAME:

PASSWORD:

NOTES:

WEBSITE:

E-MAIL:

USERNAME:

PASSWORD:

NOTES:

WEBSITE:

E-MAIL:

USERNAME:

PASSWORD:

NOTES:

WEBSITE:

E-MAIL:

USERNAME:

PASSWORD:

NOTES:

WEBSITE:

E-MAIL:

USERNAME:

PASSWORD:

NOTES:

WEBSITE:

E-MAIL:

USERNAME:

PASSWORD:

NOTES:

WEBSITE:

E-MAIL:

USERNAME:

PASSWORD:

NOTES:

WEBSITE:

E-MAIL:

USERNAME:

PASSWORD:

NOTES:

WEBSITE:

E-MAIL:

USERNAME:

PASSWORD:

NOTES:

WEBSITE:

E-MAIL:

USERNAME:

PASSWORD:

NOTES:

WEBSITE:

E-MAIL:

USERNAME:

PASSWORD:

NOTES:

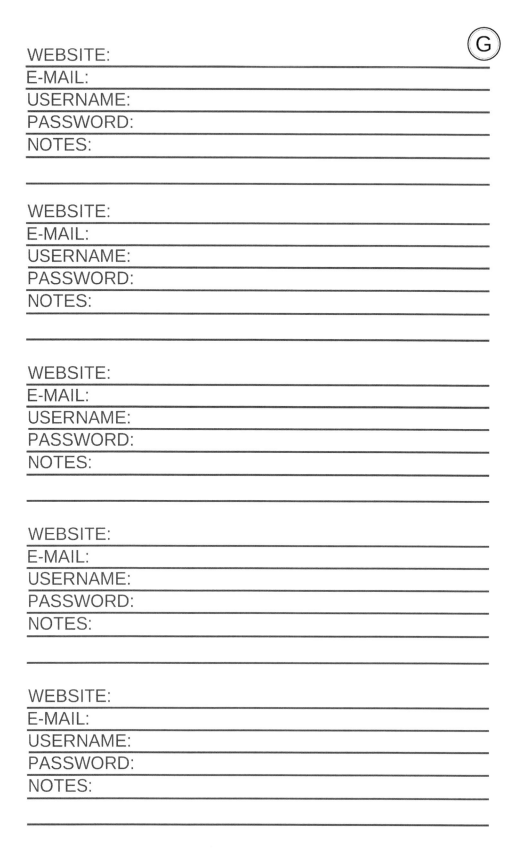

WEBSITE:

E-MAIL:

USERNAME:

PASSWORD:

NOTES:

WEBSITE:

E-MAIL:

USERNAME:

PASSWORD:

NOTES:

WEBSITE:

E-MAIL:

USERNAME:

PASSWORD:

NOTES:

WEBSITE:

E-MAIL:

USERNAME:

PASSWORD:

NOTES:

WEBSITE:

E-MAIL:

USERNAME:

PASSWORD:

NOTES:

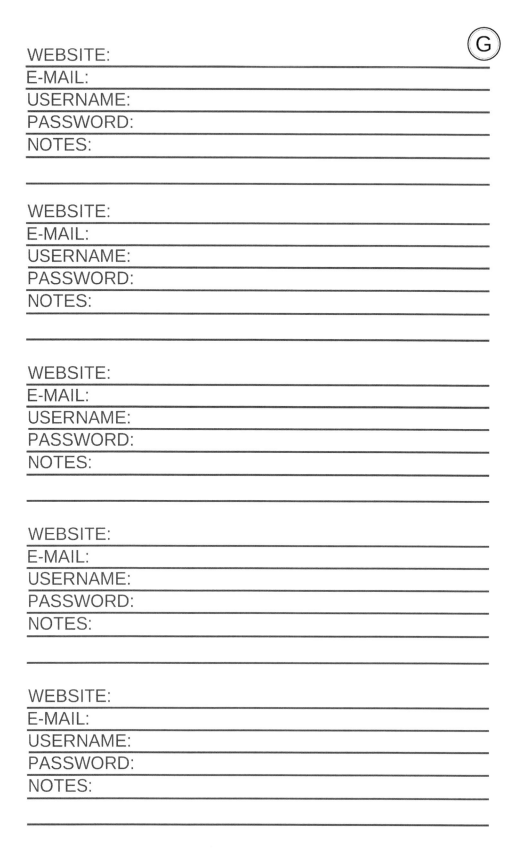

WEBSITE:

E-MAIL:

USERNAME:

PASSWORD:

NOTES:

WEBSITE:

E-MAIL:

USERNAME:

PASSWORD:

NOTES:

WEBSITE:

E-MAIL:

USERNAME:

PASSWORD:

NOTES:

WEBSITE:

E-MAIL:

USERNAME:

PASSWORD:

NOTES:

WEBSITE:

E-MAIL:

USERNAME:

PASSWORD:

NOTES:

WEBSITE:

E-MAIL:

USERNAME:

PASSWORD:

NOTES:

WEBSITE:

E-MAIL:

USERNAME:

PASSWORD:

NOTES:

WEBSITE:

E-MAIL:

USERNAME:

PASSWORD:

NOTES:

WEBSITE:

E-MAIL:

USERNAME:

PASSWORD:

NOTES:

WEBSITE:

E-MAIL:

USERNAME:

PASSWORD:

NOTES:

WEBSITE:

E-MAIL:

USERNAME:

PASSWORD:

NOTES:

WEBSITE:

E-MAIL:

USERNAME:

PASSWORD:

NOTES:

WEBSITE:

E-MAIL:

USERNAME:

PASSWORD:

NOTES:

WEBSITE:

E-MAIL:

USERNAME:

PASSWORD:

NOTES:

WEBSITE:

E-MAIL:

USERNAME:

PASSWORD:

NOTES:

WEBSITE:

E-MAIL:

USERNAME:

PASSWORD:

NOTES:

WEBSITE:

E-MAIL:

USERNAME:

PASSWORD:

NOTES:

WEBSITE:

E-MAIL:

USERNAME:

PASSWORD:

NOTES:

WEBSITE:

E-MAIL:

USERNAME:

PASSWORD:

NOTES:

WEBSITE:

E-MAIL:

USERNAME:

PASSWORD:

NOTES:

WEBSITE:

E-MAIL:

USERNAME:

PASSWORD:

NOTES:

WEBSITE:

E-MAIL:

USERNAME:

PASSWORD:

NOTES:

WEBSITE:

E-MAIL:

USERNAME:

PASSWORD:

NOTES:

WEBSITE:

E-MAIL:

USERNAME:

PASSWORD:

NOTES:

WEBSITE:

E-MAIL:

USERNAME:

PASSWORD:

NOTES:

WEBSITE:

E-MAIL:

USERNAME:

PASSWORD:

NOTES:

WEBSITE:

E-MAIL:

USERNAME:

PASSWORD:

NOTES:

WEBSITE:

E-MAIL:

USERNAME:

PASSWORD:

NOTES:

WEBSITE:

E-MAIL:

USERNAME:

PASSWORD:

NOTES:

WEBSITE:

E-MAIL:

USERNAME:

PASSWORD:

NOTES:

WEBSITE:

E-MAIL:

USERNAME:

PASSWORD:

NOTES:

WEBSITE:

E-MAIL:

USERNAME:

PASSWORD:

NOTES:

WEBSITE:

E-MAIL:

USERNAME:

PASSWORD:

NOTES:

WEBSITE:

E-MAIL:

USERNAME:

PASSWORD:

NOTES:

WEBSITE:

E-MAIL:

USERNAME:

PASSWORD:

NOTES:

WEBSITE:

E-MAIL:

USERNAME:

PASSWORD:

NOTES:

WEBSITE:

E-MAIL:

USERNAME:

PASSWORD:

NOTES:

WEBSITE:

E-MAIL:

USERNAME:

PASSWORD:

NOTES:

WEBSITE:

E-MAIL:

USERNAME:

PASSWORD:

NOTES:

WEBSITE:

E-MAIL:

USERNAME:

PASSWORD:

NOTES:

WEBSITE:

E-MAIL:

USERNAME:

PASSWORD:

NOTES:

WEBSITE:

E-MAIL:

USERNAME:

PASSWORD:

NOTES:

WEBSITE:

E-MAIL:

USERNAME:

PASSWORD:

NOTES:

WEBSITE:

E-MAIL:

USERNAME:

PASSWORD:

NOTES:

WEBSITE:

E-MAIL:

USERNAME:

PASSWORD:

NOTES:

WEBSITE:

E-MAIL:

USERNAME:

PASSWORD:

NOTES:

WEBSITE:

E-MAIL:

USERNAME:

PASSWORD:

NOTES:

WEBSITE:

E-MAIL:

USERNAME:

PASSWORD:

NOTES:

WEBSITE:

E-MAIL:

USERNAME:

PASSWORD:

NOTES:

WEBSITE:

E-MAIL:

USERNAME:

PASSWORD:

NOTES:

WEBSITE:

E-MAIL:

USERNAME:

PASSWORD:

NOTES:

WEBSITE:

E-MAIL:

USERNAME:

PASSWORD:

NOTES:

WEBSITE:

E-MAIL:

USERNAME:

PASSWORD:

NOTES:

WEBSITE:

E-MAIL:

USERNAME:

PASSWORD:

NOTES:

WEBSITE:

E-MAIL:

USERNAME:

PASSWORD:

NOTES:

(K)

WEBSITE:

E-MAIL:

USERNAME:

PASSWORD:

NOTES:

WEBSITE:

E-MAIL:

USERNAME:

PASSWORD:

NOTES:

WEBSITE:

E-MAIL:

USERNAME:

PASSWORD:

NOTES:

WEBSITE:

E-MAIL:

USERNAME:

PASSWORD:

NOTES:

WEBSITE:

E-MAIL:

USERNAME:

PASSWORD:

NOTES:

WEBSITE:

E-MAIL:

USERNAME:

PASSWORD:

NOTES:

WEBSITE:

E-MAIL:

USERNAME:

PASSWORD:

NOTES:

WEBSITE:

E-MAIL:

USERNAME:

PASSWORD:

NOTES:

WEBSITE:

E-MAIL:

USERNAME:

PASSWORD:

NOTES:

WEBSITE:

E-MAIL:

USERNAME:

PASSWORD:

NOTES:

WEBSITE:

E-MAIL:

USERNAME:

PASSWORD:

NOTES:

WEBSITE:

E-MAIL:

USERNAME:

PASSWORD:

NOTES:

WEBSITE:

E-MAIL:

USERNAME:

PASSWORD:

NOTES:

WEBSITE:

E-MAIL:

USERNAME:

PASSWORD:

NOTES:

WEBSITE:

E-MAIL:

USERNAME:

PASSWORD:

NOTES:

WEBSITE:

E-MAIL:

USERNAME:

PASSWORD:

NOTES:

WEBSITE:

E-MAIL:

USERNAME:

PASSWORD:

NOTES:

WEBSITE:

E-MAIL:

USERNAME:

PASSWORD:

NOTES:

WEBSITE:

E-MAIL:

USERNAME:

PASSWORD:

NOTES:

WEBSITE:

E-MAIL:

USERNAME:

PASSWORD:

NOTES:

WEBSITE:

E-MAIL:

USERNAME:

PASSWORD:

NOTES:

WEBSITE:

E-MAIL:

USERNAME:

PASSWORD:

NOTES:

WEBSITE:

E-MAIL:

USERNAME:

PASSWORD:

NOTES:

WEBSITE:

E-MAIL:

USERNAME:

PASSWORD:

NOTES:

WEBSITE:

E-MAIL:

USERNAME:

PASSWORD:

NOTES:

WEBSITE:

E-MAIL:

USERNAME:

PASSWORD:

NOTES:

WEBSITE:

E-MAIL:

USERNAME:

PASSWORD:

NOTES:

WEBSITE:

E-MAIL:

USERNAME:

PASSWORD:

NOTES:

WEBSITE:

E-MAIL:

USERNAME:

PASSWORD:

NOTES:

WEBSITE:

E-MAIL:

USERNAME:

PASSWORD:

NOTES:

WEBSITE:

E-MAIL:

USERNAME:

PASSWORD:

NOTES:

WEBSITE:

E-MAIL:

USERNAME:

PASSWORD:

NOTES:

WEBSITE:

E-MAIL:

USERNAME:

PASSWORD:

NOTES:

WEBSITE:

E-MAIL:

USERNAME:

PASSWORD:

NOTES:

WEBSITE:

E-MAIL:

USERNAME:

PASSWORD:

NOTES:

WEBSITE:

E-MAIL:

USERNAME:

PASSWORD:

NOTES:

WEBSITE:

E-MAIL:

USERNAME:

PASSWORD:

NOTES:

WEBSITE:

E-MAIL:

USERNAME:

PASSWORD:

NOTES:

WEBSITE:

E-MAIL:

USERNAME:

PASSWORD:

NOTES:

WEBSITE:

E-MAIL:

USERNAME:

PASSWORD:

NOTES:

WEBSITE:

E-MAIL:

USERNAME:

PASSWORD:

NOTES:

WEBSITE:

E-MAIL:

USERNAME:

PASSWORD:

NOTES:

WEBSITE:

E-MAIL:

USERNAME:

PASSWORD:

NOTES:

WEBSITE:

E-MAIL:

USERNAME:

PASSWORD:

NOTES:

WEBSITE:

E-MAIL:

USERNAME:

PASSWORD:

NOTES:

M

WEBSITE:

E-MAIL:

USERNAME:

PASSWORD:

NOTES:

WEBSITE:

E-MAIL:

USERNAME:

PASSWORD:

NOTES:

WEBSITE:

E-MAIL:

USERNAME:

PASSWORD:

NOTES:

WEBSITE:

E-MAIL:

USERNAME:

PASSWORD:

NOTES:

WEBSITE:

E-MAIL:

USERNAME:

PASSWORD:

NOTES:

WEBSITE:

E-MAIL:

USERNAME:

PASSWORD:

NOTES:

WEBSITE:

E-MAIL:

USERNAME:

PASSWORD:

NOTES:

WEBSITE:

E-MAIL:

USERNAME:

PASSWORD:

NOTES:

WEBSITE:

E-MAIL:

USERNAME:

PASSWORD:

NOTES:

WEBSITE:

E-MAIL:

USERNAME:

PASSWORD:

NOTES:

WEBSITE:

E-MAIL:

USERNAME:

PASSWORD:

NOTES:

WEBSITE:

E-MAIL:

USERNAME:

PASSWORD:

NOTES:

WEBSITE:

E-MAIL:

USERNAME:

PASSWORD:

NOTES:

WEBSITE:

E-MAIL:

USERNAME:

PASSWORD:

NOTES:

WEBSITE:

E-MAIL:

USERNAME:

PASSWORD:

NOTES:

WEBSITE:

E-MAIL:

USERNAME:

PASSWORD:

NOTES:

WEBSITE:

E-MAIL:

USERNAME:

PASSWORD:

NOTES:

WEBSITE:

E-MAIL:

USERNAME:

PASSWORD:

NOTES:

WEBSITE:

E-MAIL:

USERNAME:

PASSWORD:

NOTES:

WEBSITE:

E-MAIL:

USERNAME:

PASSWORD:

NOTES:

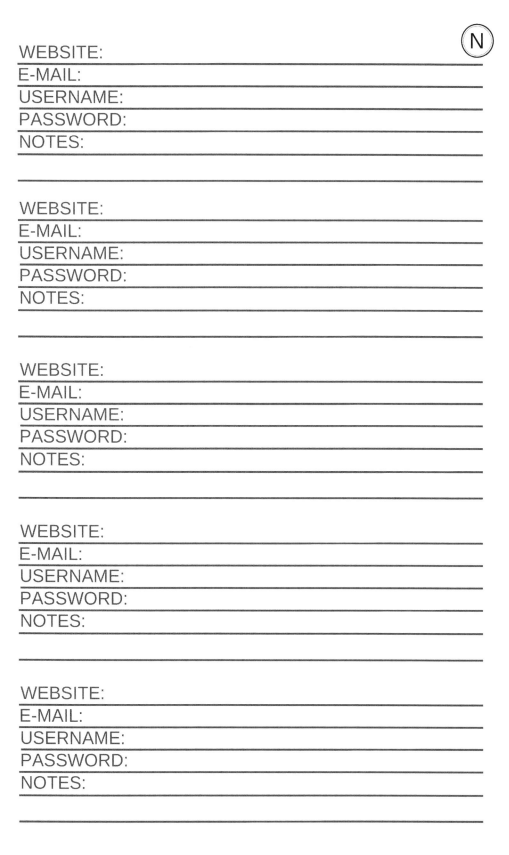

WEBSITE:

E-MAIL:

USERNAME:

PASSWORD:

NOTES:

WEBSITE:

E-MAIL:

USERNAME:

PASSWORD:

NOTES:

WEBSITE:

E-MAIL:

USERNAME:

PASSWORD:

NOTES:

WEBSITE:

E-MAIL:

USERNAME:

PASSWORD:

NOTES:

WEBSITE:

E-MAIL:

USERNAME:

PASSWORD:

NOTES:

WEBSITE:

E-MAIL:

USERNAME:

PASSWORD:

NOTES:

WEBSITE:

E-MAIL:

USERNAME:

PASSWORD:

NOTES:

WEBSITE:

E-MAIL:

USERNAME:

PASSWORD:

NOTES:

WEBSITE:

E-MAIL:

USERNAME:

PASSWORD:

NOTES:

WEBSITE:

E-MAIL:

USERNAME:

PASSWORD:

NOTES:

WEBSITE:

E-MAIL:

USERNAME:

PASSWORD:

NOTES:

WEBSITE:

E-MAIL:

USERNAME:

PASSWORD:

NOTES:

WEBSITE:

E-MAIL:

USERNAME:

PASSWORD:

NOTES:

WEBSITE:

E-MAIL:

USERNAME:

PASSWORD:

NOTES:

WEBSITE:

E-MAIL:

USERNAME:

PASSWORD:

NOTES:

WEBSITE:

E-MAIL:

USERNAME:

PASSWORD:

NOTES:

WEBSITE:

E-MAIL:

USERNAME:

PASSWORD:

NOTES:

WEBSITE:

E-MAIL:

USERNAME:

PASSWORD:

NOTES:

WEBSITE:

E-MAIL:

USERNAME:

PASSWORD:

NOTES:

WEBSITE:

E-MAIL:

USERNAME:

PASSWORD:

NOTES:

WEBSITE:

E-MAIL:

USERNAME:

PASSWORD:

NOTES:

WEBSITE:

E-MAIL:

USERNAME:

PASSWORD:

NOTES:

WEBSITE:

E-MAIL:

USERNAME:

PASSWORD:

NOTES:

WEBSITE:

E-MAIL:

USERNAME:

PASSWORD:

NOTES:

WEBSITE:

E-MAIL:

USERNAME:

PASSWORD:

NOTES:

WEBSITE:

E-MAIL:

USERNAME:

PASSWORD:

NOTES:

WEBSITE:

E-MAIL:

USERNAME:

PASSWORD:

NOTES:

WEBSITE:

E-MAIL:

USERNAME:

PASSWORD:

NOTES:

WEBSITE:

E-MAIL:

USERNAME:

PASSWORD:

NOTES:

WEBSITE:

E-MAIL:

USERNAME:

PASSWORD:

NOTES:

WEBSITE:

E-MAIL:

USERNAME:

PASSWORD:

NOTES:

WEBSITE:

E-MAIL:

USERNAME:

PASSWORD:

NOTES:

WEBSITE:

E-MAIL:

USERNAME:

PASSWORD:

NOTES:

WEBSITE:

E-MAIL:

USERNAME:

PASSWORD:

NOTES:

WEBSITE:

E-MAIL:

USERNAME:

PASSWORD:

NOTES:

WEBSITE:

E-MAIL:

USERNAME:

PASSWORD:

NOTES:

WEBSITE:

E-MAIL:

USERNAME:

PASSWORD:

NOTES:

WEBSITE:

E-MAIL:

USERNAME:

PASSWORD:

NOTES:

WEBSITE:

E-MAIL:

USERNAME:

PASSWORD:

NOTES:

WEBSITE:

E-MAIL:

USERNAME:

PASSWORD:

NOTES:

WEBSITE:

E-MAIL:

USERNAME:

PASSWORD:

NOTES:

WEBSITE:

E-MAIL:

USERNAME:

PASSWORD:

NOTES:

WEBSITE:

E-MAIL:

USERNAME:

PASSWORD:

NOTES:

WEBSITE:

E-MAIL:

USERNAME:

PASSWORD:

NOTES:

WEBSITE:

E-MAIL:

USERNAME:

PASSWORD:

NOTES:

WEBSITE:

E-MAIL:

USERNAME:

PASSWORD:

NOTES:

WEBSITE:

E-MAIL:

USERNAME:

PASSWORD:

NOTES:

WEBSITE:

E-MAIL:

USERNAME:

PASSWORD:

NOTES:

WEBSITE:

E-MAIL:

USERNAME:

PASSWORD:

NOTES:

WEBSITE:

E-MAIL:

USERNAME:

PASSWORD:

NOTES:

WEBSITE:

E-MAIL:

USERNAME:

PASSWORD:

NOTES:

WEBSITE:

E-MAIL:

USERNAME:

PASSWORD:

NOTES:

WEBSITE:

E-MAIL:

USERNAME:

PASSWORD:

NOTES:

WEBSITE:

E-MAIL:

USERNAME:

PASSWORD:

NOTES:

WEBSITE:

E-MAIL:

USERNAME:

PASSWORD:

NOTES:

WEBSITE:

E-MAIL:

USERNAME:

PASSWORD:

NOTES:

WEBSITE:

E-MAIL:

USERNAME:

PASSWORD:

NOTES:

WEBSITE:

E-MAIL:

USERNAME:

PASSWORD:

NOTES:

WEBSITE:

E-MAIL:

USERNAME:

PASSWORD:

NOTES:

WEBSITE:

E-MAIL:

USERNAME:

PASSWORD:

NOTES:

WEBSITE:

E-MAIL:

USERNAME:

PASSWORD:

NOTES:

WEBSITE:

E-MAIL:

USERNAME:

PASSWORD:

NOTES:

WEBSITE:

E-MAIL:

USERNAME:

PASSWORD:

NOTES:

WEBSITE:

E-MAIL:

USERNAME:

PASSWORD:

NOTES:

WEBSITE:

E-MAIL:

USERNAME:

PASSWORD:

NOTES:

WEBSITE:

E-MAIL:

USERNAME:

PASSWORD:

NOTES:

WEBSITE:

E-MAIL:

USERNAME:

PASSWORD:

NOTES:

WEBSITE:

E-MAIL:

USERNAME:

PASSWORD:

NOTES:

WEBSITE:

E-MAIL:

USERNAME:

PASSWORD:

NOTES:

WEBSITE:

E-MAIL:

USERNAME:

PASSWORD:

NOTES:

WEBSITE:

E-MAIL:

USERNAME:

PASSWORD:

NOTES:

WEBSITE:

E-MAIL:

USERNAME:

PASSWORD:

NOTES:

WEBSITE:

E-MAIL:

USERNAME:

PASSWORD:

NOTES:

WEBSITE:

E-MAIL:

USERNAME:

PASSWORD:

NOTES:

WEBSITE:

E-MAIL:

USERNAME:

PASSWORD:

NOTES:

WEBSITE:

E-MAIL:

USERNAME:

PASSWORD:

NOTES:

WEBSITE:

E-MAIL:

USERNAME:

PASSWORD:

NOTES:

WEBSITE:

E-MAIL:

USERNAME:

PASSWORD:

NOTES:

WEBSITE:

E-MAIL:

USERNAME:

PASSWORD:

NOTES:

WEBSITE:

E-MAIL:

USERNAME:

PASSWORD:

NOTES:

®

WEBSITE:

E-MAIL:

USERNAME:

PASSWORD:

NOTES:

WEBSITE:

E-MAIL:

USERNAME:

PASSWORD:

NOTES:

WEBSITE:

E-MAIL:

USERNAME:

PASSWORD:

NOTES:

WEBSITE:

E-MAIL:

USERNAME:

PASSWORD:

NOTES:

WEBSITE:

E-MAIL:

USERNAME:

PASSWORD:

NOTES:

WEBSITE:

E-MAIL:

USERNAME:

PASSWORD:

NOTES:

WEBSITE:

E-MAIL:

USERNAME:

PASSWORD:

NOTES:

WEBSITE:

E-MAIL:

USERNAME:

PASSWORD:

NOTES:

WEBSITE:

E-MAIL:

USERNAME:

PASSWORD:

NOTES:

WEBSITE:

E-MAIL:

USERNAME:

PASSWORD:

NOTES:

WEBSITE:

E-MAIL:

USERNAME:

PASSWORD:

NOTES:

WEBSITE:

E-MAIL:

USERNAME:

PASSWORD:

NOTES:

WEBSITE:

E-MAIL:

USERNAME:

PASSWORD:

NOTES:

WEBSITE:

E-MAIL:

USERNAME:

PASSWORD:

NOTES:

WEBSITE:

E-MAIL:

USERNAME:

PASSWORD:

NOTES:

WEBSITE:

E-MAIL:

USERNAME:

PASSWORD:

NOTES:

WEBSITE:

E-MAIL:

USERNAME:

PASSWORD:

NOTES:

WEBSITE:

E-MAIL:

USERNAME:

PASSWORD:

NOTES:

WEBSITE:

E-MAIL:

USERNAME:

PASSWORD:

NOTES:

WEBSITE:

E-MAIL:

USERNAME:

PASSWORD:

NOTES:

WEBSITE:

E-MAIL:

USERNAME:

PASSWORD:

NOTES:

WEBSITE:

E-MAIL:

USERNAME:

PASSWORD:

NOTES:

WEBSITE:

E-MAIL:

USERNAME:

PASSWORD:

NOTES:

WEBSITE:

E-MAIL:

USERNAME:

PASSWORD:

NOTES:

WEBSITE:

E-MAIL:

USERNAME:

PASSWORD:

NOTES:

WEBSITE:

E-MAIL:

USERNAME:

PASSWORD:

NOTES:

WEBSITE:

E-MAIL:

USERNAME:

PASSWORD:

NOTES:

WEBSITE:

E-MAIL:

USERNAME:

PASSWORD:

NOTES:

WEBSITE:

E-MAIL:

USERNAME:

PASSWORD:

NOTES:

WEBSITE:

E-MAIL:

USERNAME:

PASSWORD:

NOTES:

WEBSITE:

E-MAIL:

USERNAME:

PASSWORD:

NOTES:

WEBSITE:

E-MAIL:

USERNAME:

PASSWORD:

NOTES:

WEBSITE:

E-MAIL:

USERNAME:

PASSWORD:

NOTES:

WEBSITE:

E-MAIL:

USERNAME:

PASSWORD:

NOTES:

WEBSITE:

E-MAIL:

USERNAME:

PASSWORD:

NOTES:

WEBSITE:

E-MAIL:

USERNAME:

PASSWORD:

NOTES:

WEBSITE:

E-MAIL:

USERNAME:

PASSWORD:

NOTES:

WEBSITE:

E-MAIL:

USERNAME:

PASSWORD:

NOTES:

WEBSITE:

E-MAIL:

USERNAME:

PASSWORD:

NOTES:

WEBSITE:

E-MAIL:

USERNAME:

PASSWORD:

NOTES:

WEBSITE:

E-MAIL:

USERNAME:

PASSWORD:

NOTES:

WEBSITE:

E-MAIL:

USERNAME:

PASSWORD:

NOTES:

WEBSITE:

E-MAIL:

USERNAME:

PASSWORD:

NOTES:

WEBSITE:

E-MAIL:

USERNAME:

PASSWORD:

NOTES:

WEBSITE:

E-MAIL:

USERNAME:

PASSWORD:

NOTES:

WEBSITE:

E-MAIL:

USERNAME:

PASSWORD:

NOTES:

WEBSITE:

E-MAIL:

USERNAME:

PASSWORD:

NOTES:

WEBSITE:

E-MAIL:

USERNAME:

PASSWORD:

NOTES:

WEBSITE:

E-MAIL:

USERNAME:

PASSWORD:

NOTES:

WEBSITE:

E-MAIL:

USERNAME:

PASSWORD:

NOTES:

WEBSITE:

E-MAIL:

USERNAME:

PASSWORD:

NOTES:

WEBSITE:

E-MAIL:

USERNAME:

PASSWORD:

NOTES:

WEBSITE:

E-MAIL:

USERNAME:

PASSWORD:

NOTES:

WEBSITE:

E-MAIL:

USERNAME:

PASSWORD:

NOTES:

WEBSITE:

E-MAIL:

USERNAME:

PASSWORD:

NOTES:

WEBSITE:

E-MAIL:

USERNAME:

PASSWORD:

NOTES:

WEBSITE:

E-MAIL:

USERNAME:

PASSWORD:

NOTES:

WEBSITE:

E-MAIL:

USERNAME:

PASSWORD:

NOTES:

WEBSITE:

E-MAIL:

USERNAME:

PASSWORD:

NOTES:

WEBSITE:

E-MAIL:

USERNAME:

PASSWORD:

NOTES:

WEBSITE:

E-MAIL:

USERNAME:

PASSWORD:

NOTES:

WEBSITE:

E-MAIL:

USERNAME:

PASSWORD:

NOTES:

WEBSITE:

E-MAIL:

USERNAME:

PASSWORD:

NOTES:

WEBSITE:

E-MAIL:

USERNAME:

PASSWORD:

NOTES:

WEBSITE:

E-MAIL:

USERNAME:

PASSWORD:

NOTES:

WEBSITE:

E-MAIL:

USERNAME:

PASSWORD:

NOTES:

WEBSITE:

E-MAIL:

USERNAME:

PASSWORD:

NOTES:

WEBSITE:

E-MAIL:

USERNAME:

PASSWORD:

NOTES:

WEBSITE:

E-MAIL:

USERNAME:

PASSWORD:

NOTES:

WEBSITE:

E-MAIL:

USERNAME:

PASSWORD:

NOTES:

WEBSITE:

E-MAIL:

USERNAME:

PASSWORD:

NOTES:

WEBSITE:

E-MAIL:

USERNAME:

PASSWORD:

NOTES:

WEBSITE:

E-MAIL:

USERNAME:

PASSWORD:

NOTES:

WEBSITE:

E-MAIL:

USERNAME:

PASSWORD:

NOTES:

WEBSITE:

E-MAIL:

USERNAME:

PASSWORD:

NOTES:

WEBSITE:

E-MAIL:

USERNAME:

PASSWORD:

NOTES:

WEBSITE:

E-MAIL:

USERNAME:

PASSWORD:

NOTES:

WEBSITE:

E-MAIL:

USERNAME:

PASSWORD:

NOTES:

WEBSITE:

E-MAIL:

USERNAME:

PASSWORD:

NOTES:

WEBSITE:

E-MAIL:

USERNAME:

PASSWORD:

NOTES:

WEBSITE:

E-MAIL:

USERNAME:

PASSWORD:

NOTES:

WEBSITE:

E-MAIL:

USERNAME:

PASSWORD:

NOTES:

WEBSITE:

E-MAIL:

USERNAME:

PASSWORD:

NOTES:

WEBSITE:

E-MAIL:

USERNAME:

PASSWORD:

NOTES:

WEBSITE:

E-MAIL:

USERNAME:

PASSWORD:

NOTES:

WEBSITE:

E-MAIL:

USERNAME:

PASSWORD:

NOTES:

WEBSITE:

E-MAIL:

USERNAME:

PASSWORD:

NOTES:

WEBSITE:

E-MAIL:

USERNAME:

PASSWORD:

NOTES:

WEBSITE:

E-MAIL:

USERNAME:

PASSWORD:

NOTES:

WEBSITE:

E-MAIL:

USERNAME:

PASSWORD:

NOTES:

WEBSITE:

E-MAIL:

USERNAME:

PASSWORD:

NOTES:

WEBSITE:

E-MAIL:

USERNAME:

PASSWORD:

NOTES:

WEBSITE:

E-MAIL:

USERNAME:

PASSWORD:

NOTES:

WEBSITE:

E-MAIL:

USERNAME:

PASSWORD:

NOTES:

WEBSITE:

E-MAIL:

USERNAME:

PASSWORD:

NOTES:

WEBSITE:

E-MAIL:

USERNAME:

PASSWORD:

NOTES:

WEBSITE:

E-MAIL:

USERNAME:

PASSWORD:

NOTES:

WEBSITE:

E-MAIL:

USERNAME:

PASSWORD:

NOTES:

WEBSITE:

E-MAIL:

USERNAME:

PASSWORD:

NOTES:

WEBSITE:

E-MAIL:

USERNAME:

PASSWORD:

NOTES:

W

WEBSITE:

E-MAIL:

USERNAME:

PASSWORD:

NOTES:

WEBSITE:

E-MAIL:

USERNAME:

PASSWORD:

NOTES:

WEBSITE:

E-MAIL:

USERNAME:

PASSWORD:

NOTES:

WEBSITE:

E-MAIL:

USERNAME:

PASSWORD:

NOTES:

WEBSITE:

E-MAIL:

USERNAME:

PASSWORD:

NOTES:

WEBSITE:

E-MAIL:

USERNAME:

PASSWORD:

NOTES:

WEBSITE:

E-MAIL:

USERNAME:

PASSWORD:

NOTES:

WEBSITE:

E-MAIL:

USERNAME:

PASSWORD:

NOTES:

WEBSITE:

E-MAIL:

USERNAME:

PASSWORD:

NOTES:

WEBSITE:

E-MAIL:

USERNAME:

PASSWORD:

NOTES:

WEBSITE:

E-MAIL:

USERNAME:

PASSWORD:

NOTES:

WEBSITE:

E-MAIL:

USERNAME:

PASSWORD:

NOTES:

WEBSITE:

E-MAIL:

USERNAME:

PASSWORD:

NOTES:

WEBSITE:

E-MAIL:

USERNAME:

PASSWORD:

NOTES:

WEBSITE:

E-MAIL:

USERNAME:

PASSWORD:

NOTES:

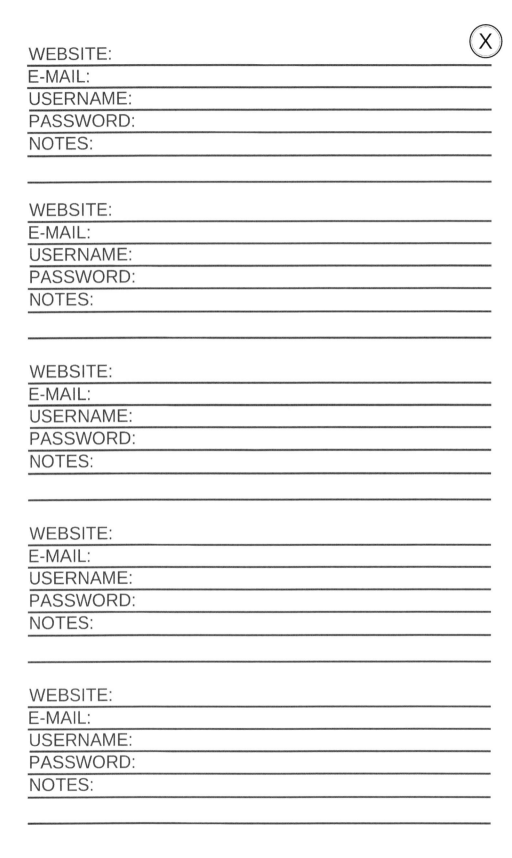

WEBSITE:

E-MAIL:

USERNAME:

PASSWORD:

NOTES:

WEBSITE:

E-MAIL:

USERNAME:

PASSWORD:

NOTES:

WEBSITE:

E-MAIL:

USERNAME:

PASSWORD:

NOTES:

WEBSITE:

E-MAIL:

USERNAME:

PASSWORD:

NOTES:

WEBSITE:

E-MAIL:

USERNAME:

PASSWORD:

NOTES:

(X)

WEBSITE:

E-MAIL:

USERNAME:

PASSWORD:

NOTES:

WEBSITE:

E-MAIL:

USERNAME:

PASSWORD:

NOTES:

WEBSITE:

E-MAIL:

USERNAME:

PASSWORD:

NOTES:

WEBSITE:

E-MAIL:

USERNAME:

PASSWORD:

NOTES:

WEBSITE:

E-MAIL:

USERNAME:

PASSWORD:

NOTES:

WEBSITE:

E-MAIL:

USERNAME:

PASSWORD:

NOTES:

WEBSITE:

E-MAIL:

USERNAME:

PASSWORD:

NOTES:

WEBSITE:

E-MAIL:

USERNAME:

PASSWORD:

NOTES:

WEBSITE:

E-MAIL:

USERNAME:

PASSWORD:

NOTES:

WEBSITE:

E-MAIL:

USERNAME:

PASSWORD:

NOTES:

WEBSITE:

E-MAIL:

USERNAME:

PASSWORD:

NOTES:

WEBSITE:

E-MAIL:

USERNAME:

PASSWORD:

NOTES:

WEBSITE:

E-MAIL:

USERNAME:

PASSWORD:

NOTES:

WEBSITE:

E-MAIL:

USERNAME:

PASSWORD:

NOTES:

WEBSITE:

E-MAIL:

USERNAME:

PASSWORD:

NOTES:

WEBSITE:

E-MAIL:

USERNAME:

PASSWORD:

NOTES:

WEBSITE:

E-MAIL:

USERNAME:

PASSWORD:

NOTES:

WEBSITE:

E-MAIL:

USERNAME:

PASSWORD:

NOTES:

WEBSITE:

E-MAIL:

USERNAME:

PASSWORD:

NOTES:

WEBSITE:

E-MAIL:

USERNAME:

PASSWORD:

NOTES:

WEBSITE:

E-MAIL:

USERNAME:

PASSWORD:

NOTES:

WEBSITE:

E-MAIL:

USERNAME:

PASSWORD:

NOTES:

WEBSITE:

E-MAIL:

USERNAME:

PASSWORD:

NOTES:

WEBSITE:

E-MAIL:

USERNAME:

PASSWORD:

NOTES:

WEBSITE:

E-MAIL:

USERNAME:

PASSWORD:

NOTES:

WEBSITE:

E-MAIL:

USERNAME:

PASSWORD:

NOTES:

WEBSITE:

E-MAIL:

USERNAME:

PASSWORD:

NOTES:

WEBSITE:

E-MAIL:

USERNAME:

PASSWORD:

NOTES:

WEBSITE:

E-MAIL:

USERNAME:

PASSWORD:

NOTES:

WEBSITE:

E-MAIL:

USERNAME:

PASSWORD:

NOTES:

WEBSITE:

E-MAIL:

USERNAME:

PASSWORD:

NOTES:

WEBSITE:

E-MAIL:

USERNAME:

PASSWORD:

NOTES:

WEBSITE:

E-MAIL:

USERNAME:

PASSWORD:

NOTES:

WEBSITE:

E-MAIL:

USERNAME:

PASSWORD:

NOTES:

WEBSITE:

E-MAIL:

USERNAME:

PASSWORD:

NOTES:

WEBSITE:

E-MAIL:

USERNAME:

PASSWORD:

NOTES:

WEBSITE:

E-MAIL:

USERNAME:

PASSWORD:

NOTES:

WEBSITE:

E-MAIL:

USERNAME:

PASSWORD:

NOTES:

WEBSITE:

E-MAIL:

USERNAME:

PASSWORD:

NOTES:

WEBSITE:

E-MAIL:

USERNAME:

PASSWORD:

NOTES:

WEBSITE:

E-MAIL:

USERNAME:

PASSWORD:

NOTES:

WEBSITE:

E-MAIL:

USERNAME:

PASSWORD:

NOTES:

WEBSITE:

E-MAIL:

USERNAME:

PASSWORD:

NOTES:

WEBSITE:

E-MAIL:

USERNAME:

PASSWORD:

NOTES:

WEBSITE:

E-MAIL:

USERNAME:

PASSWORD:

NOTES:

WEBSITE:

E-MAIL:

USERNAME:

PASSWORD:

NOTES:

WEBSITE:

E-MAIL:

USERNAME:

PASSWORD:

NOTES:

WEBSITE:

E-MAIL:

USERNAME:

PASSWORD:

NOTES:

WEBSITE:

E-MAIL:

USERNAME:

PASSWORD:

NOTES:

WEBSITE:

E-MAIL:

USERNAME:

PASSWORD:

NOTES:

WEBSITE:

E-MAIL:

USERNAME:

PASSWORD:

NOTES:

WEBSITE:

E-MAIL:

USERNAME:

PASSWORD:

NOTES:

WEBSITE:

E-MAIL:

USERNAME:

PASSWORD:

NOTES:

WEBSITE:

E-MAIL:

USERNAME:

PASSWORD:

NOTES:

WEBSITE:

E-MAIL:

USERNAME:

PASSWORD:

NOTES:

Made in the USA
Monee, IL
12 September 2021